B.R. 14300/761

WESTERN REGION
of
BRITISH RAILWAYS

HC

BRITISH TRANSPORT COMMISSION
BRITISH RAILWAYS BOARD

DIVISIONAL TRAFFIC MANAGER
(LONDON DIVISION)
PADDINGTON STATION
LONDON, W.2

G. A. V. PHILLIPS
Divisional Traffic Manager
C. F. E. HARVEY
Assistant Divisional Traffic Manager

Telephone
PADDINGTON 7000
Ext. 2794
Telegraphic Address
TRAFMAN WESRAIL
LONDON TASN
Telex No. 24126

Your Reference

Our Reference RM/1139

14th February, 1963.

C.P. Walker, Esq.,
"Chanctonbury",
5, Station Road,
THURNBY, Leicester.

Dear Sir,

Your letter of the 8th February and photographs have been passed to me by Mr. Rogers. I thank you for the photographs, which are extremely good.

It will be in order for you to visit Old Oak Common Depot at 9/0 pm on Friday, 22nd February and the necessary permit is enclosed.

I trust you will obtain s
results on this occasion and
will prove interesting and en

Yours fai

for G.A.V.

CHI

RUNNING & MAINTENANCE

---

64 Stafford Rd.
Twilight Gdns
Mudoo

Dear Colin,

Many Many Thanks for Photos which I received today 21st. I am sorry I have not answered your Carl, but I have been very busy at Cat, as Steel Main Crankshaft bearings go - but they are all O.K. again now.

Well Colin I was down sheds a week ago, Only surprised to see that Engines 5044 & 4098 are Put In Great Diesel Rd. I have been Put to cover Padd tunk? & Ran Bridge. for the time & think it is the slim edge of the Redundancy Notice but not to worry yet,

Yours Sincerely
[signature]

WESTERN REGION
STEAM TWILIGHT

PART ONE

Frontispiece. *The seafront at Dawlish is already filling up with holiday makers as 'Castle' No 5028 'Llantisilio Castle' pauses in the station on its way to Plymouth with the early morning 5.30am express from Paddington to Penzance. 2.8.57.*

WESTERN REGION STEAM TWILIGHT

Part One

Colin Walker

PENDYKE PUBLICATIONS

INTRODUCTION

This is the first of five books covering the last years of Western Region steam. Each book will contain a different selection of photographs but they will all follow a similar sequence of routes. Beginning with London and routes to the West Country the albums then take in Sapperton Bank in the Cotswolds before moving to Oxford and the main line to Worcester. This route saw the last of the regular 'Castle'-hauled expresses. Oxford also became one of the final strongholds of Western steam and was the last Western steam depot to close. The routes the depot served to Worcester and north-westwards to Banbury, Birmingham and beyond in London Midland territory were slow to be dieselised. Because of the author's strong links with these lines and also his residence in Oxfordshire during the final chapter of Western engine steam working each book will give the routes to Banbury and the north west a particularly strong emphasis.

As with his previous books in the Steam Twilight series the author has not confined his photography to fine weather. Trains did not stop running in rain, snow, fog or when the light faded. Also, if a long distance was travelled in order to obtain photographs at a special spot and the weather deteriorated it had to be accepted. True much detail might not be apparent but what was lost could perhaps be more than made up by 'atmosphere'.

The author wishes to acknowledge the generous help and facilities provided by both the Western and London Midland Regions of the former British Railways. He also expresses his gratitude to the enginemen who admitted him to their footplates, the railway staff of all grades who supported his endeavours either officially or by conniving and turning a 'blind eye'.

Then there were the workshop, factory and shop owners like the proprietor of Messrs Edwards', the button manufacturer in Park Street, Birmingham and the manager of Nortons departmental store in nearby Moor Street who both allowed him onto their rooftops. Also the flour mill foreman in Bath who admitted him on to his mill roof on the Lower Bristol Road. Their kindness and co-operation was not wasted.

On a more spiritual level he remembers with reverent appreciation the Rectors of St.James's church, Somerton in Oxfordshire and St. Andrew's church, Shifnal in Shropshire for permission to climb to the top of their church towers. Then there was Ronald Brown, farmer of Somerton in Oxfordshire who allowed the author the freedom to roam his fields and finally the late Jack Nash, carpenter, joiner jobbing builder and signalman at Heyford. With his wife Alice he lived next door to the author in Somerton and his brash but generous neighbourliness is warmly remembered.

ISBN 0904318 17 6

© Colin Walker 1997

Published by:
Pendyke Publications,
'Gorffwysfa',
Methodist Hill,
Froncysyllte,
Llangollen,
Wrexham.
LL20 7SN

Tel/Fax 01691 778180

Photoset in North Wales by Derek Doyle & Associates, Mold, Flintshire.
Printed by the Amadeus Press Ltd., Huddersfield, W. Yorkshire.

PADDINGTON AND OLD OAK COMMON

It was perhaps because of a liking for solitude that I rarely photographed steam at the London termini, preferring instead to shun the crowds and take shots of engines 'under way' with their trains. This was especially so where a climb and some heavy exhaust was on offer as on the gradients out of Kings Cross and Euston. An exception to this habit was the odd photograph I obtained during my nocturnal footplate trips into Marylebone on the Great Central with Leicester crews when an hour or two's turn-round time allowed a fleeting visit to another station.

My shots at Paddington of 'Castle' No 5057 'Earl Waldegrave' heading the night mail to Penzance were taken on such an occasion on St. Valentine's night in February 1959 when I had travelled up to London on the 4.5pm from Manchester.

Other, more substantial nocturnal assignments were the two visits I paid to Old Oak Common shed in February and October 1963 when steam was still alive but in rapid decline. I chose the times of the year carefully to ensure a long period of darkness and deliberately used the depot's normal lighting to bring out the softness and subtleties of light and shadow which are often lost with the use of flash.

Night-time has an 'enclosing' effect on objects that are artificially illuminated. Forms are stressed differently from their daylit appearance when surrounding features and extraneous detail play a far more conspicuous part. Similarly, it was not so much a compliance with any regulation but more of a psychological instinct that made engine movements and even shunting seem more restrained during the sleeping hours. At an engine shed the tasks of engine positioning, movement, servicing and refuelling which went on all night appeared to be undertaken so much more discreetly and quietly than the same activities during the day.

Long camera exposures at night did however bring with them the hazards of unwelcome drifts of haze, steam and smoke that could beat down upon the camera when they were not expected. Droplets of vapour could cloud the lens with some ghastly consequences and ripe language would then ensue.

Many moods were evident at night at Old Oak. They ranged from the 'family', almost conversational atmosphere inside the shed where engines clustered round the turntables in an interior and sometimes pungent haze; to the shed roads outside where engines stood beneath the high flood lights prepared for the road and awaiting their crews and their time; to the shed's main line pilot usually standing alone ready to cover any failure; to the well-lit occupants of the coaling stage road waiting to receive their tonnage of Welsh coal; to the equally well-lit ashpit road where fires were trimmed or thrown out; and finally to the melancholy of the 'dead' line whose occupants of past glories were waiting to be towed away for scrap.

The two visits to Old Oak were very different. On the first occasion in February many of the engines were still cared for and pleasantly clean including those on the condemned line. However, by October a spirit of dejection and neglect was only too obvious and paintwork once glistening was more often than not covered in grime. Pride had given way to despair. Nevertheless, engines still wore their nameplates and cabside numbers which, as these books will show, was more than the remnants of Western steam did on the lines north of Oxford two years later.

My two nights spent among the engines at Old Oak Common were undertaken with official permission for which I shall always be grateful. Equally remembered and appreciated was the kindness and cooperation of shed staff like Running Foreman Fred Hext and Bill Dorey who moved engines around for me and placed them on the turntable so that I could photograph them at my leisure as they stood proudly alone. Such kindness stirs the warmest of memories.

Finally, any comment on Old Oak Common shed cannot fail to mention the excellent canteen where, following one's labours with the camera, an appetising and substantial hot meal could be obtained at a very reasonable and probably subsidised price. Such perks were more than welcome on a cold night.

Following Pages
2. *With its headboard reversed a Bristol Bath Road 'Castle' No 5057 'Earl Waldegrave' which had earlier worked in the up 'Merchant Venturer' prepares to return home from Paddington with the 11.50pm night express to Penzance via Bristol. 14.2.59*

3. *A Cardiff Canton 'Britannia' Pacific No 70016 'Ariel' hurries away from Paddington and passes the station at Westbourne Park with the down 'Capitals United Express'.*

4. *Old Oak Common Nocturne. Bill Dorey, one of the night shed staff at Old Oak Common does a check on 'Castle' No 5041 'Tiverton Castle' as she stands on one of the roundhouse roads. 22.2.63.*

5. *On a Winter evening in February 1963 a 'Grange' No 6829 'Burmington Grange' and 2-8-0 No 2873 stand ready prepared to work the 8.55pm freight to Margham and the 10.40pm to Weymouth respectively. 22.2.63.*

6. No 5098 'Clifford Castle' in somewhat scruffy condition has been moved onto the turntable in Old Oak Common shed so that its portrait can be taken. The camera and tripod are down in one of the engine pits. 19.10.63.

7. A long exposure taken through the glass of one of the windows on the office block stairway at Old Oak Common catches 'Hall' No 6912 'Helmster Hall' which is being prepared to work the 11.35pm freight to Cardiff. 22.2.63.

'Earl of St.Germans' sets off for Paddington with the
4.0pm express from Cheltenham. 14.6.61.

out of the up loop and on to the main line at Swindon
with an up parcels train. 14.6.61.

10. A Pannier tank No 8714 skurries past Sidney Gardens in Bath with an up mixed freight consisting of a van, a wagon and a brake van. 8.7.61.

11. On a sunny, summer afternoon in 1961 a shopkeeper on the Lower Wells Road allowed me to take some photographs from the small roof windows which looked onto the railway at the back of his premises. Here, a 'Hall' No 6994 'Baggrave Hall' sets off from Bath with the 2.35pm express from Paddington to Bristol and Weston Super Mare via Devizes. 16.6.61.

Following Page

12. *A photograph taken from the roof of the flour mill on the other side of the line on the Lower Bristol Road sees 'Castle' No 5061 'Earl of Birkenhead' heading for Bristol with the 4.15pm express from Paddington to Plymouth via Bristol. 16.6.61.*

13. *The author's train is slowed by signals as it approaches Taunton thus allowing time to snatch a shot of 'Castle' No 5062 'Earl of Shaftesbury' which is hurrying eastwards with the 11.0am from Newquay to York. 30.8.58.*

14. *A Mogul No 9315 trundles quietly up Rattery Bank with two milk tanks, two parcels vans and three vans. 4.9.58.*

15. A 'Castle' No 5052 'Earl of Radnor' heads for Kingswear along the single line from Torquay with the 11.10am stopping train from Exeter St. Davids. It will return on the 1.50pm express to Paddington. 2.8.57.

16. The signalman at Tigley box on Rattery Bank gives the driver of 'Castle' No 5024 'Carew Castle' a wave of encouragement as he climbs past unassisted with the down 'Cornishman' from Wolverhampton to Penzance. No 5024 is obviously in fine fettle. 4.9.58.

17. Sapperton Bank. On a murky morning on the 17th February 1961 a 0-4-2 tank No 1426 pauses at St. Mary's Crossing Halt with the 8.42 am auto train from Stonehouse to Chalford.

18. The local trains between Swindon and Cheltenham were frequently used as a running-in turn for engines after their overhaul at Swindon works. Here on a misty July morning in 1962 a well presented 'Hall' No 6985 'Parwick Hall' calls at Chalford on its way down the gradient with the 7.58am local train from Swindon to Cheltenham. 13.7.61.

Previous Page

19. *This photograph is one of my personal favourites. As I describe in my essay on the Cotswolds I often associated certain parts of the country with a particular class of engine and the Cotswolds for me were inseparable from the Great Western 'Castles'. The landscape and engine were a perfect compliment to each other. For Cheltenham-Paddington trains the lift out of the Severn valley through Stroud and up the delightfully named Golden Valley into Sapperton tunnel was a tough climb with steepening gradients of 1 in 75, 74,60, and finally 90 inside the tunnel.*

In late April 1962 I had journeyed to the line near Frampton Crossing to obtain a shot of a 'Castle' climbing the bank with the 5.38pm train from Cheltenham to Swindon. It was a beautiful evening.

The train approached first within earshot and then view but then to my dismay so also did the late running down 'Cheltenham Spa Express' which drifted cautiously down the grade headed by 'Castle' No 7000 'Viscount Portal'.

It was quite obvious that the coaches of the long down train would block out the climbing 'Castle' I had come to photograph and with an accompanying torrent of 'ripe' expletives that was perhaps incompatible with the serenity of the evening I fired off a desperate shot of the two engines as they were about to distantly pass each other. Ramming the slide back into the plate holder and continuing to curse my luck I departed the scene in high dudgeon.

It was only when I developed the film that I realised what a piece of visual poetry I had captured with No 7000 whistling a greeting to No 7033 'Hartlebury Castle' which was climbing past. The gleaming boilers of both engines reflecting the late evening sun made for a perfect spectacle. Certainly the shot I had originally planned would never have provided such a dramatic result. 26.4.62.

20. *In a Cotswold drizzle after its transfer from from the up line to the down at Chalford, No 1426 is ready bunker first to propel the single-coach 9.30am auto train through to Gloucester 17.2.61.*

21. *Another shot of No 1426 standing in the down platform at Chalford with the 9.30am auto train for Gloucester. Driver Roy Hill looks out. 17.2.61.*

Oxford to Worcester.

22. In the lengthening shadows of a summer evening a 'Castle' No 7025 'Sudeley Castle' passes Hinksey Yard on its way into Oxford with the down 'Cathedrals Express'. The cessation of engine cleaning on the Western was a sad break with a fine tradition. Western engines with their copper and brass ornamentation demanded a polish and cleanliness that added an essential dignity to their looks. Also, the sparkle of gleaming metal and paintwork helped to create a photograph that was much richer in contrast than an engine that was scruffy as here. 5.7.63.

23. In Platform 1 which was the down bay at Oxford a locally based 'Hall' No 7911 'Lady Margaret Hall' waits to leave with the 1.25pm stopping train to Worcester. 6.7.63.

24. A rain-soaked moment at Oxford finds 'Castle' No 7027 'Thornbury Castle' standing in the down platform with the 1.15pm express from Paddington to Worcester. In the other direction a 'Hall' No 6992 'Arborfield Hall' approaches with the 1.10 pm from Worcester to Paddington. 6.7.63.

25. On the same day 'Castle' No 7029 'Clun Castle' pulls out of Oxford in the rain with the 11.15am express from Paddington to Worcester. The crew who have darkened the sky in answer to a request for some smoke look out for the camera. 6.7.63.

26. 'Castle' No 7027 'Thornbury Castle' again this time pulling away from Oxford past the engine shed with the 3.15pm express from Paddington to Worcester and Hereford.

27. *Snow is lying in the fields on a winter afternoon in March 1963 as 'Castle' No 7023 'Penrice Castle' climbs into the Cotswolds up the valley of the Evenlode towards Charlbury with the 1.15pm from Paddington to Worcester. 2.3.63.*

28. After calling at Charlbury on an afternoon of winter sunshine, a 'Hall' No 4979 'Wootton Hall' sets off with the 1.25pm local train from Oxford to Worcester. 2.3.63.

29. Up and down near Aston Magna. A 'Hall' No 5952 'Cogan Hall' running light engine towards Oxford passes 'Castle' No 7025 'Sudeley Castle' which is heading a Paddington–Worcester express. 8.6.63.

31. A 'Grange' No 6813 'Eastbury Grange' heads an up train of empty wagons near Aston Magna between Chipping Campden and Moreton in Marsh. 18.5.63.

Previous Page
30. On an afternoon of sunshine in mid March a 'Castle' No 7004 'Eastnor Castle' pulls out of Kingham with the 11 15am express from Paddington to Worcester and Hereford. 16.3.63.

32. *Passing the brick and tile works at Aston Magna on the same day is 'Castle' No 5031 'Totnes Castle' with the 11.15am express from Paddington to Worcester.*

THE COTSWOLDS

If there was an area of England which had a special association with a class of locomotive it was surely the Cotswolds with the Western 'Castles'. The routes to Paddington from Plymouth and Exeter via Castle Cary and Birmingham over the Bicester 'cut off' may have been dignified by the 'Kings' but the four Cotswold routes belonged essentially to the 'Castles' at least until the appearance of the 'Britannia' Pacifics on the expresses from South Wales in 1952.

All the Cotswold routes involved tunnels through the west facing scarp but each line possessed its own special characteristics. The southern-most line was, of course, Brunel's original main line to London from Bristol through Bath, a city which more than any other displayed the glory of Cotswold stone as a building material. By utilising the valley of the Bristol Avon almost as far as Bathford and then its tributary the By Brook it managed to reach the village of Box before meeting any serious gradient to climb. Then 2½ miles first at 1 in 120 quickly steepening to 1 in 100 saw trains through the short Middle Hill tunnel and then the 1 mile 1452 yards long Box tunnel after which it was easy running again on to Chippenham and a return to the Avon valley.

Ten miles to the north of Box tunnel another main line tunnelled through the Cotswolds near the town of Chipping Sodbury. This was the main line from South Wales via the Severn tunnel and was also the alternative and preferred route for expresses from Bristol to Paddington. After a punishing climb out of Bristol trains made their approach to the Cotswold escarpment and Sodbury tunnel over longer and easier gradients to the summit near Badminton. Over 11 miles of climbing was kept to a reasonable gradient of 1 in 300 which imposed little strain on an engine and once over the top there followed a descent also at 1 in 300 for nearly 10 miles. It was over this favourable stretch where 'Castles' heading the up 'Bristolian' nudged speeds of three figures and where the Bristol Bath Rd. 'Castle' No 7018 'Drysllwyn Castle' attained them with a recorded feat of 102 miles an hour. Both routes from Bristol joined at Wootton Bassett six miles from Swindon.

The next Cotswold climb 17 miles further north reached the mouth of Sapperton tunnel. This was on the line from Cheltenham and Gloucester and it involved the heaviest climb of all four routes and was perhaps the most scenic. After some flat running south from Gloucester along the Severn Valley as far as Standish Junction trains then turned eastwards and approached the Cotswold escarpment through Stonehouse to Stroud beyond which town the climb to the tunnel at Sapperton began in earnest. After passing Brimscombe where a banking engine was kept in steam the last 3½ miles were pretty grim with gradients of 1 in 103,75,70,74,75,60 and finally 1 in 90 inside the tunnel. As the line climbed up the Golden Valley past Brimscombe, Chalford and Frampton Mansell it twisted and turned as it kept company both with the erstwhile Severn and Thames Canal and also the River Frome until the latter turned northward when both canal and railway were forced to tunnel beneath the wolds. The summit of the railway climb was reached towards the east end of the 2 mile 924 yard tunnel after which it was downhill for most of the way to Swindon.

The most northerly of the Cotswold main lines was the route from Worcester to Oxford and Paddington. The south eastern exit from the 887 yard Campden tunnel was within a mile of the medieval 'wool' town of Chipping Campden and it came near the end of a six mile climb out of the Vale of Evesham. The 17 or so miles of easy running over the vale from Worcester did however give engines time to get well warmed up before the climb began and the approach to the tunnel was made through an avenue of trees planted to screen the railway and its trains from the local landowner who was obviously not a railway enthusiast.

The descent from Campden was not a simple one. Instead, after 1½ miles of falling gradient to the village of Blockley trains found themselves climbing again out of the dip created by the Knee Brook for 2½ miles past Aston Magna to a final summit near Moreton in Marsh. After that it was all gently downhill to Oxford and the Thames along the valley of the lovely River Evenlode.

As with similar limestone country like that around Stoke Bank on the East Coast main line in South Lincolnshire, the Cotswolds were a benevolent landscape with long, sweeping, rounded hills where the colour of its stone walls and buildings and the soils underlying its grasses and crops cheerfully reflected the light. In short, on a fine day the Cotswolds smiled.

Of the four Cotswold routes, my photography was concentrated on the two northerly climbs to the Sapperton and Campden tunnels where a serious effort was demanded of engines and a good boiler was a useful asset. The Worcester main line also possessed the added attractions of its lingering use of steam and its accessibility to my then home in the Midlands. This enabled me to spend a few hours on the line at many different locations.

34. *Emerging from Campden Tunnel a 'Hall' No 4955 'Plaspower Hall' heads for Oxford with a train of pipes forming the morning freight from Pontypool Road. 8.6.63.*

33. *Another 'Castle' No 7004 'Eastnor Castle' dashes round the curve past milepost 93¾ between Blockley and Aston Magna with an up express from Worcester to Paddington.*

35. *At the other end of the Campden tunnel a 'Castle' No 5042 'Winchester Castle' hurries out with the 9.15am express from Paddington to Worcester and Hereford. 21.8.62.*

36. *Approaching Honeybourne under easy steam is 'Castle' No 4082 'Windsor Castle' which is descending Campden bank with the 12.45pm express from Paddington to Worcester and Hereford. 2.8.60.*

... Castle ... passes ... and begins the climb out of the Vale of Evesham towards the Cotswolds with the 12.5pm from Hereford to Paddington. 21.8.62.

makes a competent climb of Campden bank with the 12.55pm express from Worcester to Paddington. 2.8.60.

40. Dirty but unbowed. Inside Worcester shed a 'Castle' No 7027 'Thornbury Castle' is being prepared to work the Eastleigh parcels. 21.8.63.

fine backdrop to this shot of 2-8-0 No 3856 which is bringing a short freight along the line from Hereford past the engine shed and towards Tunnel Junction. 21.8.63.

41. *Engine change. A 'Hall' No 6924 formerly 'Grantley Hall' arrives with a Summer holiday train from the north and prepares to hand over to Southern 'West Country' Pacific No 34040 'Crewkerne' which is standing alongside.*

42. *A 'Hall' No 6904 'Charfield Hall' sets off from Oxford with the 8.30 am summer through train from Newcastle to Bournemouth. 6.7.63.*

43. On its last legs a 'Hall' class No 6964 formerly 'Thornbridge Hall' looks to be in a sorry external condition as it sets off from Oxford with the York- Poole through train.

44. Also leaving Oxford is 'Manor' No 7824 'Iford Manor' with the 10.30am from Birmingham to Eastbourne and Hastings. 20.7.63.

45. *After being held up outside Oxford station a 'Hall' No 6981 'Marbury Hall' gets the road into Platform 2 with a holiday extra from the South Coast. Waiting in the up siding is 'Battle of Britain' Pacific No 34085 '501 Squadron' which is waiting to take over the southbound*

46. *Passing Oxford's fine gasholders is locally based 'Hall' No 7911 'Lady Margaret Hall' with an interesting mixed freight which includes steel girders, wagons of coal and petrol tankers. 5.7.63*

Following Page
47. *A 'Hall' No 7908 'Henshall Hall' pulls out of Platform 3 with the 8.35am from Birmingham Moor Street to Portsmouth and Southsea. 20.7.63.*

48. *Losing not a little steam a 'Castle' No 7019 'Fowey Castle' prepares to leave Oxford station with the 9.5am express from Birkenhead to Poole. 20.7.63*

49. *Gathering speed on its way out of Oxford is 'Grange' No 6831 'Bearley Grange' heading a Summer Saturday extra from Wolverhampton to Portsmouth.*

50. Wearing class A headlamps the Great Western Society's preserved Prairie tank No 6106 passes Hinksey yard with a single coach special.

51. The towers and spires of Oxford and the Thames meadows provide a backdrop to Mogul No 7327 which is passing Hinksey yard with an up freight train. 5.7.63

52. In heavy rain a 'Hall' No 7926 'Willey Hall' is held impatiently in Platform 3 at Oxford with the 8.43am train from Margate to Wolverhampton while a failed diesel set is removed from the down main line. 6.7.63.

53. Oxford shed with 'Castle' No 7014 'Caerhays Castle', a 'Hall' and a 2-6-2 Tank No 6111 in residence.

55. Oxford shed yard on a busy Summer Saturday with Stanier 'Black 5's and 8Fs; Standard 4 4-6-0s; a Western 28xx 2-8-0; 'Hall' and 'Grange' 4-6-0s as well as Prairie and Pannier tanks. Remarkably, there does not seem to be a Southern Pacific in sight.

Following Pages

54. An overview of Oxford shed which was a rather minimal wooden structure and hardly compatible with the architectural splendour of the city. Present are Western diesel No D1008 'Western Harrier'; a 2-8-0 No 2865 and 'Hall' No 4975 'Umberslade Hall'. 20.7.63.

56. *Front ends at Oxford shed. 'Hall' No 6924 'Grantley Hall' and Prairie tank No 6145.*

57. *Smoke by request. 'Castle' No 7012 'Barry Castle' neglected, unkempt but still imperious pulls away from Oxford with the 9.28am from Bournemouth West to Manchester.*

55. In the other direction a 'Grange' No 6811 'Cranbourne Grange' hurries into Oxford with the 11.18am local train from Banbury. 12.1.63.

56. Some very wintry conditions assail 'Hall' No 6998 'Burton Agnes Hall' which is running late with the Northbound 'Pines Express'. She is seen passing Oxford shed. 12.1.63.

60. A Shrewsbury Standard 5 No 73096 is heading a northbound parcels train near Wolvercote Junction on its way out of Oxford. It is about to pass beneath the line from Bletchley which linked up with the Worcester line at Wolvercote thus bypassing Oxford.

61. Taking the line to Banbury and Birmingham at Wolvercote Junction is a 'Grange' No 6823 'Oakley Grange' with a down freight.

62. Descending Tackley 'Bank' a 'Manor' No 7808 formerly 'Cookham Manor', hurries north with a down freight train.

63. This photograph of the preserved 'Castle' No 4079 'Pendennis Castle' standing impatiently blowing off steam at Heyford illustrates the audacity of my neighbour, Jack Nash. The engine was en route from Didcot to Tyseley one Sunday morning when Jack was duty signalman. He knew from his special notices that it was running, of course, and I was informed well in advance. When the 'Castle' arrived at Heyford it found the down starter against it and despite some protestive whistles the signal remained obstinately 'on'. Drawing to a stop the crew watched somewhat astounded as the signalman descended from his box and took a wander of inspection round the engine. Then, having satisfied his own curiosity and checking that all necessary photographs had been obtained by the privileged 'hangers on' he shouted to the crew that they could continue their journey and to ignore the signals which were still at danger. So, No 4079 ambled off in the sunshine breaking numerous regulations as it did so.

65. *Another nameless 'Hall' No 6944, formerly 'Fledborough Hall' dashes through Heyford with the Poole-York express. Stowed in the loop is the local DMU bound for Banbury.*

Previous Page
64. *The Walker family are forced to participate in a photograph of 'Hall' No 6934 formerly 'Beachamwell Hall' which is climbing Tackley bank between Heyford and Bletchington with an up mixed freight train.*

SOMERTON

On a Summer afternoon in 1949 I stepped from a train at Heyford station on the Western Region line between Banbury and Oxford. I was in R.A.F. uniform and, having handed in my travel warrant, boarded the basic, bench-seated Bedford 'Garry' for the journey to R.A.F. Upper Heyford. As a newly trained Radio Telephony Operator I had been posted to the airfield to serve the greater portion of my National Service. At that time Upper Heyford was No 1 Parachute and Glider School and a part of Transport Command.

After the allocation of a bunk and locker in the Signals Section billet, I was attached to one of the National Service 'old hands' and taken out in the 'garry' to the airfield's Direction Finding Station, or 'homer'. This involved a journey of some three miles along country roads past the villages of Upper Heyford and Somerton. It was at Somerton that the Bedford briefly employed low gear and climbed onto the limestone scarp where it dropped it's passengers on a quiet country lane that looked out over the Cherwell valley across crops and pastures to distant towers and spires. The vista also took in the watery 'ribbons' of the river and the Oxford Canal while far-off creeping 'threads' of steam marked the two Western rail routes from Oxford and from Bicester which joined at Aynho Junction.

The 'homer' was a small, wooden, hexagonal structure that tapered towards a point in the roof through which a revolveable aerial protruded. It stood on a concrete base inside a fence in the middle of a barley field belonging to Farmer Brown of Somerton. When it was not involved with local flying Upper Heyford Homer provided a continuous distress watch. It never switched out. At night or on quiet days it was just possible to feel the rumble of trains as they passed beneath the adjacent field through Ardley tunnel which was on the direct route from London via Bicester.

Other interests crowded my young life in 1950 but I did occasionally take a Coronet box camera and wander down through the pastures belonging to old Mrs Irons at nearby Hill House Farm to the tunnel mouth where I took blurred snapshots of 'Kings', 'Castles', 'Halls' and the odd 28er as they dashed out of the tunnel and into the Cherwell Valley. I still have them suitably hidden away!

My demob took place on the last day of July 1950. I was unofficially conveyed back to Heyford station in the Bedford 'garry' accompanied by a group of well-wishers who came to see me off. Things had changed dramatically at Upper Heyford. All our R.A.F. planes had been dispatched to other airfields and the United States Air Force had moved in. Their plans for expansion would almost dwarf the original airfield as would their massive aircraft. Little did I realise then that I would one day be seeing quite a lot of them.

My journey home to Leicester was through Banbury and on to the Great Central at Woodford. It was a link that was to play a vital role in the future when I set about photographing the last of Great Central line and Western steam.

It was fifteen years after my demob that I returned to Somerton but this time it was to take up residence in a 17th Century stone and thatched house which looked down over another of Farmer Ronald Brown's fields and onto the Western main line to Oxford.

The landscape around Somerton proved to be particularly helpful when it came to photographing steam. The rolling limestone country combined with the line's twists and turns as it kept company with the River Cherwell and the Oxford Canal offered a variety of settings to choose from both above and below track level.

Sadly though, the move to Somerton coincided with the steady demise of Western steam. However, though the names of engines and their numerical identities were gradually stripped from them and the splendour of their brass, copper and paintwork was lost beneath a patina of grime, many of them went out in fine, dynamic style.

During the last two years of steam over the line from Oxford I must have taken hundreds of photographs of freight and passenger trains and particularly the York-Poole express and its balancing working. Being resident close to the railway I was able to enjoy it at all times of the day and at night. Those enthusiasts who have to read on photographs the numbers of engines and count the rivets would not approve of the pleasure I gained from leaning against the railway fence at night and watching the dark shapes of engines and their trains as they passed. The only lights would be those of sparks from chimneys, headlamps, fireholes and gauge-glass lamps in cabs and finally tail lamps unless it was a passenger train when a whole broken ribbon of light would follow the engine. The visual pleasure would be completed by those of sound and smell.

The sounds of Western steam could also invade the bedroom. On a warm summer night when all the windows were open to catch any breeze, the distant sounds and sometimes whistles of trains passing Aynho Junction would drift in upon the ear. If, after an interval, the sound suddenly stopped one knew that the train had taken the Bicester route and entered Ardley tunnel but if it was on the Oxford line the sound of its approach and passing was long-lasting and full of 'detail'.

My residence in Somerton was well known to many engine crews particularly at Banbury and some distinctly pungent smokes were provided as they passed the village particularly on the York-Poole express. Indeed, there were possibly one or two local folk who actually welcomed the arrival of the diesels!

A final bonus to the Walker family's sojourn in Somerton was in the person of our next door neighbour. His name was Jack Nash and he was a brash, blunt, 'immediate' character and quite a law unto himself. He was also one of the signalmen at Heyford and there appeared to be few rules and regulations that met with his respect. His lack of delicacy and refinement had to be stoicly accepted as a price to be paid for his warm but brusque brand of neighbourliness.

One overslept or stayed in bed too long at one's peril! If Jack was at home and not 'on shift' and the curtains in the Walker household were still drawn it was not unusual for him to ring a handbell over the wall and shout in his rich Oxfordshire dialect, 'Come on Gaffer – Time you were up!'.

Jack travelled to work at Lower Heyford in his Ford Popular. His speed never exceeded 25 miles an hour and the car occupied the middle of the road. I cannot remember anyone ever overtaking him. They couldn't. 'When I learned to drive', he once said, 'We didn't have to bother with these ridiculous driving tests and rules'.

Both Jack and his wife Alice were wonderful neighbours and they are remembered with great affection.

Somerton

66. *In this evening shot in late August a 'Hall' No 6906 'Chicheley Hall' shuts off steam as it approaches Somerton from the South with the 3.2 pm Summer train from Portsmouth Harbour to Bristol, shot 29.8.61.*

67. *A shot from the towpath of the Oxford Canal sees a grimy and nameless 'Hall' heading towards Somerton with the Poole-York through train.*

68. *Another photograph of the the Poole-York express catches 'Hall' No 6999 formerly 'Capel Dewi Hall' hurrying round the curve approaching Somerton*

69. *From the down side of the line another 'Hall' No 6956 formerly 'Mottram Hall' approaches Somerton with the northbound Poole-York express*

More 'Granges'.

70. On an afternoon of Winter sunshine a 'Grange' No 6859, formerly 'Yieusley Grange' looks to be in good external condition and is going

71. A 'Grange' stripped of all obvious identity approaches Somerton

72. With its number chalked on the buffer bar and in a deplorable condition a 'Grange' No 6853, formerly 'Morehampton Grange' is making heavy weather of the up York-Poole express as she passes Somerton on an August afternoon in 1962.

73. A 'Hall', No 7919 formerly 'Runter Hall' passes Grays Field at Somerton with the 8.49am train from Banbury to Oxford on a morning of Summer sunshine.

18. Rebuilt Bulleid 'Pacific' 34054 is running late as she passes Somerton with a holiday extra bound for the South Coast. On the distant horizon is the tower of Deddington parish church.

heads south past Somerton with a southbound coal train.

76. *Another 'Hall' No 6934, formerly 'Beachamwell Hall' puts up a dark trail as she speeds past Somerton with the up York-Poole express.*

77. *A day of Winter sunshine sees a 'Hall' hurrying south past the Rectory field at Somerton with a mixed freight.*

Following Page
78. *An evening mist covers the Cherwell water meadows at Somerton as a 9F 2-10-0 hurries south towards Oxford with a train of flat wagons.*

79. A shot taken from the Rectory Field at Somerton catches a 9F and two 8Fs wandering northwards light to Banbury. After the closure of Oxford shed in January 1963 processions like this became quite a common sight.

80. Another 9F 2-10-0 brings a train of coal and four cement wagons through Somerton on the up road bound for Oxford.

81. *The fireman of another unidentified 'Hall' is filling the boiler as his engine speeds past Somerton with the up*

82. *A fine 'Hall' effort on the up York-Poole express rounding the curve approaching Somerton station. No 7904, formerly 'Fountains Hall' defies its almost disreputable condition by putting up a magnificent and hard-working display.*

83. Passing the signal box at Somerton
with a northbound freight is 2-8-0 No

84. A shot of the Poole-York express taken from the tow path of the
Oxford canal at Somerton catches Standard 5 4-6-0 No 73171 coasting

88. Between Aynho and Somerton a 1' Frame tank No 6111 heads the 4.18pm local train from Banbury to Oxford. Across the meadows can be seen one of the Souldern viaducts carrying the direct route from Paddington through Bicester. The two lines link up at Aynho Junction. September 1964.

89. ... travelling past the signal box with the down Poole-Bournemouth express and observing a Permanent Way speed restriction is an unidentified 'Hall' class 4-6-0.

87. *Between the station and junction at Aynho a 'Hall' No 4932 'Hatherton Hall' brings a down freight along the line from Oxford. Beyond the engine is the down line from Paddington which has crossed the Oxford line on a flyover and is descending to join it. 22.8.64.*

88. *Birmingham Snow Hill-Paddington direct. A 'King' No 6022 'King Edward 111' coasts round the curve at West Wycombe with the 8.50am from Birkenhead to Paddington. August 1962.*

89. In the afternoon sunshine No 7019 'Fowey Castle' ambles up the gradient to Saunderton and approaches Bradenham with the 4.15pm from Paddington to Banbury. August 1962.

90. The 4.15pm from Paddington to Banbury provided a rather menial task for some of the last steam locomotives at Old Oak Common. At Bicester where it arrived at 5.56pm it was moved forward along the down loop and held clear of the station to await the arrival and departure of the 5.10pm express from Paddington to Wolverhampton. Then, after reversing back into the down platform it finally left for Banbury at 6.18pm. This 22 minute stop was long enough to obtain some interesting night shots and this one shows 'Castle' No 5042 'Winchester Castle' waiting in the Bicester loop. On the down main line the 5.10pm diesel hauled express from Paddington is signalled.

91. *Night photography was not without its amusements. This study of 'Grange' No 6848 'Toddington Grange' waiting in the Bicester loop with the 4.15pm from Paddington to Banbury involved some unorthodox, if not bizarre illumination. Instead of the normal flash bulbs a sixpenny Brocks 'Volcano' firework was placed inside a large, catering size jam tin which had been cut out on one side to allow out a wide spread of light. The tin was nailed to a brush stale and when the firework was lit the tin was held aloft and carried along the length of the engine and tender. The camera shutter was kept open for the duration of this 'performance' and then closed after the 'Volcano' had spluttered out. As for the engine crew . . .*

92. *Having reversed back into the platform a 'Hall' No 6951 'Impney Hall' stands in Bicester North Station with the 4.15pm from Paddington to Banbury.*

Previous Page
93. A 'Hall' No 6938 'Corndean Hall' looks to be in fine condition as she waits in the loop at Bicester with the 4.15pm from Paddington to Banbury.

94. A familiar performer on the 4.15pm from Paddington was 'Castle' No 7029 'Clun Castle' seen here standing in the loop during its wait.

95. A 9F No 92074 climbs through the limestone cutting approaching Ardley with a northbound train of car flats.

96. *Waiting to leave the quarry sidings at Ardley with the Harbury cement stone train is double chimney 9F 2-10-0 No 92227.*

97. *Under way and on the climb to Ardley Tunnel No 92227 makes light work of the stone train bound for Greaves's siding which served Harbury Cement works.*

98. Climbing to Ardley tunnel from the south is a 'Hall' which has been stripped of all identity. It is heading a

99. Before its preservation No 7029 'Clun Castle' climbs the 1 in 200 to Ardley Tunnel with an MRS special to Swindon via London on a misty

100. At the end of the day a 'Hall' has steam to spare as it makes a casual climb over one of the Souldern viaducts with the 5.50pm from Birmingham Snow Hill to Paddington. October 1964.

101. A photograph taken from the Oxford line between Aynho and Somerton catches a 'Castle' climbing to Ardley tunnel on the main Bicester line with the evening 5.50pm express from Birmingham Snow Hill to Paddington. September 1964

Following Page
102. Another shot taken from the Oxford line catches 'King' No 6019 'King Henry V' with brakes biting hard as it dashes down to Aynho Junction with the 3.10 pm express from Paddington to Wolverhampton. 15.6.62

...ing at speeds up to around a high-speed soaking time trying to around a high-speed soaking was not always easy. 'Castle' No 5091 'Cleeve Abbey' has the scoop well down in the water trough at Aynho as it dashes towards Banbury with the 8.45am from Margate to Wolverhampton during a stormy moment on an August day in 1964. 22.8.64

stone train waits on the flyover to join the down Oxford-Banbury line at Aynho Junction.

105. In the other direction but under clearer skies a 'Grange' also has the scoop in as it heads for Oxford with the 9.45am from Birkenhead

106. Bloxham for length, Adderbury for strength and Kings Sutton for beauty is a North Oxfordshire saying about the three churches that straddle the Cherwell valley south of Banbury. In this photograph the exquisite spire of Kings Sutton church rises in the background as a 'Hall' which has been stripped of all obvious identification hurries towards Banbury with the Poole–York 'Bearley Grange' No 6831

107. Another 'Hall' No 6927 'Lilford Hall' accelerates away from Banbury and approaches Astrop with the up York-Poole express.

Banbury

108. Having changed engine crews and taken water in the down loop at Banbury a 'Hall' No 5992 'Horton Hall' pulls out with the Tavistock-Woodford freight on a frosty afternoon in March 1963.

109. *Taking the up slow line out of Banbury another 'Hall' heads a southbound mixed freight.*

110. Frost covers the sleepers on an April day in 1963 as a 'complete' 'Hall' No 6991 'Acton Burnell Hall' vigorously leaves Banbury on the up slow line with a freight. March 1963.

111. A 'Great Western Society Special' makes a steamy start from Banbury headed by a 'Manor' No 7808 'Cookham Manor'.

112. On a misty day a Standard Class 5 4-6-0 races through Banbury with a southbound special.

114. *The time is 2.37pm by the station clock as 'Hall' No 6964, formerly 'Thornbridge Hall' stripped of its nameplates and liberally covered with filth prepares to set off from Banbury with the up York-Poole express. July 1965*

113. *Making a powerful departure from Banbury along the up slow line is 'Grange' No 6858 'Woolston Grange' with an up freight train.*

115. *Down freights in the loop at Banbury. 'Hall' No 7917 'North Aston Hall' has charge of a fitted van train while L.M. 8F No 48450 heads a mixed freight.*

116. *Banbury shed. A line up of Western engines with 'Grange' No 6827, formerly 'Llanfrechfa Grange', 'Hall' No 6947 formerly 'Helmingham Hall' and an unidentified 'Hall' are being prepared for duty. This was probably the last time a parade of Western engines was seen at Banbury and the depressing condition of the engines only added to the doom laden atmosphere at the depot. May 1965.*

117. *Shapes inside the shed. A 'Hall' represents a brief Western survival at Banbury shed among all the London Midland and Standard types after the transfer of the depot to the London Midland Region. June 1966.*

118. *Coaling up Western fashion at Banbury. August 1966.*

Previous Pages

119. *The change of ownership is apparent again in this picture of L.M. 8F 2-8-0 No 48220 and 9F No 92013 which have replaced the Western engines outside the shed at Banbury. The habit of scrawling reporting numbers on smokebox doors however seems to persist. August 1966.*

120. *A night contemplation at Banbury shed of 9F 2-10-0 No 92223 which is standing prepared and ready for work.*

121. *A young Walker takes a look at the original Standard 5 No 73000 outside the shed at Banbury.*

122. *A double chimney 9F 2-10-0 No 92234 is being prepared at Banbury shed on a Spring morning in 1966.*

123. A grim sight alongside the shed at Banbury where James Friswell, the local scrap dealer who purchased a number of engines for scrap was authorised to cut them up on _____ of 'Hall', red and 'Black 5s are being reduced to 'scrapable' sizes

124. To revive some cheer, here is a shot of No 6020 'King Henry IV' racing non stop through Banbury with the 2.10pm express from Paddington to Birkenhead. 15.6.62.

125. *In the other direction another 'King' No 6005 'King George II' pulls out of Banbury station with the 8.55am from Birkenhead to Paddington. No 6005 looked rather shabby and soon afterwards went to Swindon works for a shopping. It was the last 'King' to receive a major overhaul. 30.7.59.*

126. A 9F 2-10-0 No 92234 pulls out of the up yard North of the station at Banbury with a heavy southbound freight. September 1966

127. Leamington driver Frank Burridge at work on 'Grange' No 6864 'Dymock Grange' which is about to leave Banbury with the 1.4pm train from Oxford to Leamington. 11.4.59.

128. Taking the S. & M.J. line at Fenny Compton a 'Hall' No 6945 'Glasfryn Hall' heads for Woodford and the G.C. main line with a train of bogie bolsters loaded with rails. 5.10.63.

130. *Also under a heavy downpour 'Hall' No 4954 'Plaish Hall' heads an up coal train towards Banbury. It is about to pass beneath the overbridge carrying the S.& M.J. line south of Fenny Compton. 5.10.63.*

129. *In a heavy shower another 'Hall' No 4964 'Rodwell Hall' approaches Fenny Compton with the 4.8pm from Birmingham to Paddington via Oxford. 11.4.59.*

Following Page

131. *Descending from the north west end of Harbury tunnel a 'Castle' No 5038 'Morlais Castle' heads the 9.20am from Bournemouth West to Wolverhampton. 28.7.62.*

Leamington Spa

132. A 'Hall' No 5983 'Henley Hall' gathers speed out of Leamington with the Summer Saturday 10.10am from of Leamington.

133. A 'Mogul' No 6366 is pressed into service on a Summer Saturday and heads a heavy train of Southern stock bound for the South Coast. It is seen passing the engine shed on its way out of Leamington.

134. *Also leaving Leamington for Paddington is 'King' No 6018 'King Henry VI' with the up 'Inter City'. 4.8.60.*

135. *Climbing away from Leamington is 'King' No 6005 'King George II' with the 8.55am from Birkenhead to Paddington. 30.7.59.*

136. *In splendid condition a 'Castle' No 5061 'Earl of Birkenhead' stands in the up platform at Leamington with the Birkenhead-Bournemouth through train.*

137. *The fireman of 'King' No 6021 'King Richard II' looks back and checks his train as he leaves Leamington with the down 'Cambrian Coast Express' 13.4.62.*

Following Page
138. *A 'King' No 6026 'King John' pulls out of Leamington with the up 'Cambrian Coast Express'. 13.4.62*

139. Hatton Bank. The five mile climb out of the Leam/Avon valley provided some pleasant sights and sounds when steam ruled the railway. Here, a 'King' No 6018 'King Henry VI' climbs Hatton Bank on a day of glorious August sunshine with the 12.10pm express from Paddington to Birkenhead. 11.8.62.

140. Earlier in the year a 'Castle' No 7036 'Taunton Castle' approaches the top of the big 'lift' to Hatton with a football special bound for the Hawthorns and the West Bromwich-Tottenham Hotspur cup tie. 17.2.62.

141. On the other side of the line on the same day a 'King' No 6015 'King Richard III' heads the down 'Inter City' near the same spot.

142. A 'Hall' No 5933 'Kingsway Hall' leaves Stratford on Avon with the 9.10am summer train from Wolverhampton to Torquay, Paignton and Kingswear .2.8.60.

143. A 'Castle' No 7024 'Powis Castle' climbs the 1 in 75 to Wilmcote after calling at Stratford on Avon with the Summer Saturday 7.40am from St. Austell to Birmingham Moor Street.

Birmingham

144. A local rush hour service, the 5.44pm from Tyseley to Wolverhampton, sets off from Bordesley and passes beneath the London Midland line to Camp Hill and Kings Norton. It is headed by 'Grange' No 6806 'Blackwell Grange'. 20.8.60.

Following Page

145. On a grey August morning a 'Hall' No 6930 'Aldersey Hall' with cylinder drains open and a very moist exhaust heads past Moor St. station in Birmingham with a down fitted freight. 22.8.61.

149. *A Summer Sunday evening finds 'County' Class 4-6-0 No 1013 'County of Dorset' moving out of Birmingham Snow Hill with the 4.10pm express from Paddington to Birkenhead. 31.7.60.*

148. *The Southbound 'Cornishman' hurries out of Snow Hill Tunnel in Birmingham and crosses over the London Midland approaches to New Street tunnels. It is headed by 'Castle' No 5031 'Totnes Castle'. 22.8.61.*

150. *Heading a Talyllyn Railway special through the tunnels leading out of Birmingham Snow Hill. No 6000 'King George V' passes through a pool of sunlight as it accelerates towards Hockley.*

151. *The 12½ miles of curved and undulating track with its numerous speed restrictions between Wolverhampton and Birmingham Snow Hill provided a useful opportunity for engines on the Paddington expresses which had started fresh from Wolverhampton to do some warming up. Here, 'King' No 6020 'King Henry IV' brings the 8.55am Birkenhead-Paddington express round the sweeping curve approaching West Bromwich. 24.8.61.*

152. A 'Prairie' tank No 5192 pauses at Old Hill with a long distance stopping train – the 2.25pm from Cardiff to Birmingham. 27.7.59.

153. A shot through, the rather dirty cab spectacle glass of Pannier tank No 6418 which is approaching Cradley Heath with the 5.45pm train from Stourbridge Junction to Old Hill. 27.7.59.

Wolverhampton Low Level

154. A 'Castle' No 5085 'Evesham Abbey' sets off from Wolverhampton on a grey morning with the 10.50am [...] *Messrs [...] 23.8.62.*

155. A top link Wolverhampton Stafford Road crew, Driver Freddie Griffiths and his fireman Gareth Jones, both fine Welshmen, on 'King' No 6008 'King James II' working the 11.45am Sunday express from Birkenhead to Paddington, 20.8.61.

156. *I always enjoyed photographing 'Kings' and 'Castles' as they emerged from the overbridge at the end of Wolverhampton Low Level station. Here a 'King' No 6022 'King Edward III' sets out for Paddington with the 8.50am express from Birkenhead. 23.8.62.*

157. *The crew of 'Castle' No 5065 'Newport Castle' take a good look at the camera as they wait in the middle road at Wolverhampton for the up 'Cambrian Coast Express' to arrive from Shrewsbury. 31.7.59.*

158. *A special train was run from Wolverhampton to Swindon on Sunday September 9th 1962 to commemorate the end of the reign of 'Kings' on the Wolverhampton-Paddington expresses. Appropriately No 6000 'King George V' was the chosen engine and here it is before departure. 9.9.62.*

159. A 'Britannia' Pacific No 70042 'Lord Roberts' draws to a stop in Wolverhampton low level ready for a crew change. It is heading a car train from Morris Cowley at Oxford to Bathgate in Scotland. Standing alongside in the down bay platform is a 'County' class 4-6-0 No 1008 'County of Cardigan' with the 4.55pm train to Chester. 22.8.63.

160. Sign of the times. A 'Western' diesel No D1002 'Western Explorer' double heads 'Castle' No 5046 'Earl Cawdor' out of Wolverhampton. They are hauling the 9.10am express from Paddington to Birkenhead. 22.8.62.

161. Standing beside the coaling plant at Stafford Road shed. Wolverhampton is 'Castle' No 7035 'Taunton Castle'. It is being re-fuelled ready to work the up 'Inter City' to Paddington. 24.8.61.

162. *Stafford Road shed was entering its last days when this photograph of 'Castle' No 7012 'Barry Castle' was taken. It is being prepared to work the 3.30pm express from Wolverhampton to Paddington. 20.8.63*

163. *A 'County' Class 4-6-0 No 1022 'County of Northampton' approaches Oakengates tunnel with a train from Shrewsbury to Wolverhampton.*

164. *Shrewsbury Passed Fireman Eddie Edwards on 'Castle' No 4090 'Dorchester Castle' which is heading a train for Wolverhampton peers through the cab window to check a signal for his driver.*

165. *A 'King' No 6021 'King Richard II' sets off from Wellington with the 2.40pm express from Birkenhead to Paddington. 23.8.62.*

166. *A keen, dull and misty afternoon in February 1959 sees 'Castle' No 5001 'Llandovery Castle' setting off from Shrewsbury round the curve to Wellington and Wolverhampton with the 11.45am express from Birkenhead to Paddington.*

167. *Another Shrewsbury crew, Driver Jack Hodnet and his fireman Ray Brookfield, on 'Castle' No 5095 'Barbury Castle' which is working the 4.30pm from Birkenhead to Paddington. 6.7.62.*

Following Page
168. *A Shrewsbury 'Castle' No 5095 'Barbury Castle' proudly rounds the curve past Severn Bridge Junction signal box with the up 'Cambrian Coast Express' and passes 'Manor' No 7803 'Barcote Manor' which had brought the train in from Aberystwyth. The express reversed at Shrewsbury and this photograph conceals a remarkable effort on the part of the signalmen at the boxes at each end of Shrewsbury station who between them managed to get the 'Manor' off the train; back through the station; turned on the triangle and into the engine siding before No 5095 pulled out. This photograph is a tribute to their wonderful co-operation. 25.8.61.*

169. An Old Oak Common 'King' No 6023 'King Edward II' sets out from Shrewsbury with the up 'Cambrian Coast Express'. 9.5.59.

170. A 'Hall' No 6934 'Beachamwell Hall' has arrived in platform 7 at Shrewsbury with the 2.45pm express from Birkenhead to Paddington. After uncoupling it moves off the train and makes for the shed. 24.8.63.

Following Pages

171. A photograph taken from the station tower at Shrewsbury finds a 'Castle' No 5092 'Tresco Abbey' waiting in Platform 4 with the 8.20am Summer Saturday train from Paddington to Pwllheli. The line to Crewe can be seen curving off to the right and the line to Chester continuing ahead of the train with the climb from Coton Hill to Leaton clearly conspicuous. 25.8.62.

172. Entering Shrewsbury from the Chester line a 'Castle' No 5081 'Lockheed Hudson' is given menial employment on a Southbound freight train. It is crossing over the line from Crewe. 6.7.62.

174. Another 'Hall' No 4979 'Wootton Hall' pulls out of Shrewsbury with the 9.30am from Bournemouth West to Birkenhead and descends the short gradient to Coton Hill before attacking the climb to Leaton. 9.5.59.

173. In heavy rain and under laden skies a 'Hall' No 4964 'Rodwell Hall' looking quite disreputable arrives in Platform 3 at Shrewsbury with the 2.10pm express from Paddington to Birkenhead. 23.8.62.

176. A Mogul No 7313 takes the line to Barmouth at Llangollen Junction, Ruabon with the 10.10am train from Paddington to Pwllheli which had changed engines and reversed at Ruabon. 23.6.62.

175. North end trio. A Western 'Hall' No 6981 'Shervington Hall' waits in Platform 4 with the 2.10pm from Paddington to Birkenhead while 'Britannia Pacific' No 70053 'Moray Firth' stands at the head of the 8.0am from Newquay to Manchester. In the middle road a 'Jubilee' No 45618 'New Hebrides' waits to take over the 10.45am from Kingswear to Manchester. 25.8.62.

177. *Passed Fireman Ray Fowles at work on 'Hall' No 6934 'Beachamwell Hall' which is hauling the 8.30am Saturday train from Cardiff to Llandudno. This train was involved in a reversal at Chester. 24.8.63.*

178. *No 6934's fireman Harold Preston puts another shovelfull of coal on the fire. Harold was a willing and cheerful young fireman who tragically died of a heart attack at the early age of 26. He is not forgotten.*

180. A 'County' Class 4-6-0 No 1013 'County of Dorset' chatters past Gresford Halt with the 2.40pm from Birkenhead to Paddington. 23.3.62.

179. A Talyllyn Railway special train climbs away from Llangollen Junction near Ruabon towards Acrefair headed by two 'Manor' Class 4-6-0s Nos 7827 'Lydham Manor' and 7822 'Foxcote Manor'. 28.9.63.

181. Return to Shrewsbury. The local depot's pride and joy, 'Castle' No 5038 'Morlais Castle' in wonderful condition stands alongside near relation No 5024 'Carew Castle' from Newton Abbot which had failed at Shrewsbury earlier in the week. It will return home as pilot to No 5038 on the 9.10am from Liverpool to Plymouth which was a lodging turn for Shrewsbury crews. 6.7.62

182. The Shrewsbury station pilot No 1016 'County of Hants' is pressed into service assisting 'Castle' No 4080 'Powderham Castle' up the climb to Church Stretton with the heavily loaded 12.20pm express from Manchester to Plymouth. Unfortunately, a surplus of steam from No 1016 effectively obliterated the 'Castle'. 23.8.61.

183. *Shrewsbury Passed Fireman Eddie Edwards at work driving 'Grange' No 6814 'Enborne Grange' which is working the 2.15pm Sunday train from Shrewsbury to Newport. 9.9.62.*

184. *In a rather disreputable condition a 'Castle' No 7011 'Banbury Castle' climbs the 1 in 100 to Church Stretton from Shrewsbury with the 12.10pm express from Manchester to Plymouth. 8.6.60.*

185. The fireman of 2-8-0 No 2892 approaching Ludlow from the south with a mixed freight watches the functioning of his engine's injector.

The Central Wales Line
186. Approaching Coleham on the way out of Shrewsbury with the 2.50pm train to Swansea Victoria via the Central Wales line is a Standard Class 5 4-6-0 No 73091. 23.8.61.

187. A Collet 0-6-0 No 2222 undertakes banking duties on the Central Wales Line from Knighton to Llangunllo. It is seen making for Knucklas and the start of the 1 in 60 climb.

188. A lineside shot of No 2222 banking a Class H freight up the Heyop valley through one of the rock cuttings between Knucklas and the summit at Llangunllo on the Central Wales Line.

Following Page
The Cambrian Line
189. Every engine seemed to have its moment at Shrewsbury. Here, a 'Manor' No 7823 'Hook Norton Manor' having taken over the down 'Cambrian Coast Express' proudly sets out for Aberystwyth. Over in No 1 Bay platform a 'Black Five' No 45283 heads a train for Swansea over the Central Wales line. 6.7.62.

191. Another shot of the up 'Cambrian Coast Express' leaving Shrewsbury hauled by 'Manor' No 7828 'Odney Manor'. It is crossing Abbey Foregate bridge. 22.8.63.

190. Collet 0-6-0 No 3205 waits in No 5 bay at Shrewsbury with the 6.30pm train for Aberystwyth as 'County' class 4-6-0 No 1017 'County of Hereford' moves off to the shed after bringing in the, 4.30pm express from Birkenhead to Paddington. 25.8.62.

192. No 7828 'Odney Manor' again heading the down 'Cambrian Coast Express' but without its headboard takes the Cambrian route out of Shrewsbury and passes Meole Brace. 31 7 64.

193. 'Manors' up and down. No 7812 'Erlestoke Manor' enters Newtown with a train from Aberystwyth and meets relation No.7823 'Hook Norton Manor' which is waiting to proceed on the single line with the 3.55pm from Shrewsbury to Aberystwyth. 25.8.61.

195. A Standard Class 3 2-6-2 tank No 82036 assists 'Manor' No 7803 'Barcote Manor' over the summit of Talerddig with the up 'Cambrian Coast Express'. 26.8.61.

194. Another 'Manor' No 7803 'Barcote Manor' coasts down the gradient from Talerddig and approaches Carno with the up 'Cambrian Coast Express'.

197. *Drifting down the bank from Talerddig with the 9.45am from Whitchurch to Aberystwyth is a Standard 4 2-6-4 tank No 80132.*

196. *Breasting the same summit is 'Manor' No 7819 'Hinton Manor' with the 12.35pm express from Aberystwyth to Crewe. 26.8.61.*

199. *On the climb between Commins Coch Halt and Llanbrynmair a Collet 0-6-0 No 2255 assists 'Manor' No 7801 'Anthony Manor' up the climb to Talerddig with the 10.55am from Aberystwyth to Manchester. 26.8.61.*

198. *Also coasting down the gradient from Talerddig with a short westbound freight on a dull morning is 'Manor' No 7801 'Anthony Manor'.*

200. *Having combined the Aberystwyth and Pwllheli portions of the up 'Cambrian Coast Express' at Dovey Junction, 'Manor' 4-6-0 No 7803 'Barcote Manor' awaits its assistant engine Class 4 4-6-0 No 75026 before setting off for Shrewsbury. 23.5.61.*

201. *A Standard Class 3 2-6-2 tank No 82006 tackles the stiff climb from Fairbourne on the Barmouth estuary up to the Friog with the 10.25am from Pwllheli to Dovey Junction. 25.5.61.*

202. A Standard Class 4 4-6-0 No 75026 takes the curve onto Barmouth bridge over the Mawddach estuary with the Pwllheli portion of the up 'Cambrian Coast Express'. 27.5.61.

203. Another Standard 4 4-6-0 No 75004 passes the quarry near Minffordd with the Pwllheli portion of the down 'Cambrian Coast Express'. 26.5.61.

Following Page

204. The evening shadows are lengthening as a Collet 0-6-0 crosses the Glaslyn valley and approaches Portmadoc with the 3.28pm from Ruabon to Pwllheli. 20.5.61.

205. *The Last train of the day from Pwllheli to Barmouth crosses the Glaslyn estuary on its way out of Portmadoc on a serene May evening. It is headed by a Standard 3 2-6-2 tank. The mountains of Cnicht, Moelwyn and Moelwyn Bach provide a backdrop. 26.5.61.*

Table 163

Table 163 — LONDON, OXFORD, KINGHAM, EVESHAM and WORCESTER

WEEK DAYS

For Notes, see page 301

Table 163 — WORCESTER, EVESHAM, KINGHAM, OXFORD and LONDON

WEEK DAYS

THE CATHEDRALS EXPRESS

For Notes, see page 303